Everything Publishing

The ultimate publishing guide

AWARD-WINNING ENTREPRENEUR
KAREN MC DERMOTT
Founder of Serenity Press

Copyright © 2019 Karen Mc Dermott

All rights reserved. No part of this book may be used or reproduced by any means, graphic, electronic, or mechanical, including photocopying, recording, taping or by any information storage retrieval system without the written permission of the copyright owner except in the case of brief quotations embodied in critical articles and reviews.

Making Magic Happen books may be ordered through online booksellers or by contacting:
hello@karenmcdermott.com.au

Because of the dynamic nature of the Internet, any web addresses or links contained in this book may have changed since publication and may no longer be valid. The views expressed in this work are solely those of the authors and do not necessarily reflect the views of the publisher and the publisher hereby disclaims any responsibility for them.

Although the author and publisher have made every effort to ensure that the information in this book was correct at press time, the author and publisher do not assume and hereby disclaim any liability to any party for any loss, damage, or disruption caused by errors or omissions, whether such errors or omissions result from negligence, accident, or any other cause.

ISBN: (sc) 978-0-6484000-1-1

ISBN: (e) 978-0-9946337-6-7

This book is dedicated to all author-publishers.

It takes many strengths to be an author-publisher
and I admire all of you greatly.
Here's to your unwavering success.

Acknowledgements
Those special people who make it all happen!

I have been blessed with many amazing people who have journeyed alongside me on my business of publishing journey. If you don't see your name on these pages but have been part of this crazy adventure please know that I will wake up in the middle of the night with a hot sweat when I remember that I forgot to add your name. So here it goes...

To my children, Dylan, Eithen, Kiera, Saoirse, Eimear and Mary, I am grateful for you every day. To Kieran, thank you.

Huge love to my mum and dad who always believe in me and everything I do and who unconditionally love us all.

To my sister Emma who is always there, no matter what.

To my sister Lisa and my three brothers who grew up alongside me, cheer me on and love my kids.

To Donna Di Lallo, your belief and support are always there and I will forever be grateful.

To Monique Mulligan for being a gorgeous part of my publishing journey. Our friendship is special to me.

To Teena Raffa-Mulligan who is the most kind and giving editor and friend.

To Tess Woods, thank you for our friendship. It is magical beyond belief.

To ALL of my authors who gift me the pleasure of joining you on your publishing journey.

To ALL of my illustrators who bring words to life through imagery.

To ALL of my readers...you rock beyond belief!

To all of the author-publishers who I have the pleasure of mentoring.

To everyone on my team at Serenity Press, MMH Press and the Everything Publishing Academy.

To Natasha Solomun for taking our authors on your books.

To Ida Janssen for designing beautiful covers and interiors.

To Joanne Fedler for our beautiful connection and for being inspiring.

To Jennifer Sharp and Peta Flanigan for believing in yourselves and allowing me to join you on your journey.

And to everyone I have yet to meet on this crazy journey.

Thank you for helping me make magic happen.

Foreword

Peace Mitchell
Ausmumpreneur & The Women's Business School

So many people dream about becoming authors and that magical day when they'll see their book in a bookshop, but for so many people this dream remains exactly that – a 'dream'. The task can seem so daunting and overwhelming – there are so many unknowns and so many questions ... but not anymore.

This book is filled with everything you need to know to get you started on your journey to becoming a published author.

Karen has helped teach hundreds of people how to publish their books and now she brings this knowledge together to help many more. She loves writing and encouraging people to not be afraid to share their story. Karen is especially passionate about inspiring people to make magic happen in their lives and I'm so delighted that you've taken the step to create magic in yours by reading this book.

Peace Mitchell
FOUNDER
THE WOMEN'S BUSINESS SCHOOL

photo: Diana Henderson @lifeasart

about the AUTHOR

Award-winning publisher, author and advanced Law of Attraction practitioner, Karen McDermott, is a sought-after publisher and speaker who shares her knowledge and wisdom on building publishing empires, establishing yourself as a successful author-publisher and writing books.

Having built a highly successful publishing business from scratch, signing major authors, writing more than 20 books and establishing her own credible brand in the market, Karen has developed strategies and techniques based on tapping into the power of knowing to create your dreams.

Karen is a gifted teacher who inspires others to make magic happen in their lives through utilising her power of knowing strategies.

Karen is the Founder of Serenity Press, the Making Magic Happen Academy, the Everything Publishing Academy and Karenmcdermott.com.au.

In 2018 she also founded her first magazine, *Enrich, everyone has a story to share* and looks forward to producing two annual publications, filled with numerous heart-centred life stories in partnership with Joanne Fedler Media.

The author of the best-selling book *Mindful Magic*, Karen's creative endeavours have seen her produce a large list of titles written across many genres, including non-fiction, fiction, children's and educational books.

She is a regular contributor to smallville.com.au and is a faculty member for the Million Dollar You Academy. She has appeared in many news publications through interviews and articles and is one of YMag's Top 10 Women to Watch in 2019.

Karen was a finalist in the 2018 Irish Chamber of Commerce awards, winner of the 2016 Ausmumpreneur excellence award and more recently both of her businesses were listed in the Anthill magazine Top 100 cool companies.

Karen has been proactive in assisting many publishing presses to become established, including Joanne Fedler Media, BOOQ Press, White Light Publishing House, Gumnut Press, Daisy Lane Publishing and The Kind Press.

Karen enjoys working with high calibre publishers and authors to create successful storytelling platforms and brands through harnessing the power of magic, infinite possibility and knowing.

about
This book

To ensure that you receive the highest possible outcome from reading this book I have divided it into two parts.

Part One is filled with industry information so that you can embark on your own publishing journey filled with knowledge and a go-to guide for publishing your book. If you want to branch out into building your own publishing empire, this section will also provide you with the know-how to make that happen.

Part Two is my story of how I have built a publishing empire in five years. I have written this from a personal perpective in the hope that you can connect easier to my story and be inspired through my passion for the written word and what fuels my desire to help more and more stories get out into the world.

To your publishing success!

Karen x

The only PUBLISHING GUIDE you'll need

Do you want to publish a book and position it in front of your target audience? This is the only guide you'll ever need.

This is not just another self-publishing guide book that teaches you how to get your book to print. While that may be highly valuable information, the purpose of this book is to encourage and enable you to take action.

It is a hands-on resource designed by widely renowned publisher Karen McDermott to inspire and educate you in the initial steps you need to take if you are serious about publishing and/or building your own publishing press.

So what makes this book DIFFERENT?

You'll get the most from this book by taking what you feel applies to your journey and implementing it to your success story.

You'll also learn:

• The basic skills you need to publish a book with access to global distribution.

• How to distribute your book to bricks and mortar bookstores.

• How to be resourceful, while still having impact.

• How to raise the vibration of your book before launch.

• How to offset your print run to maximise profits.

• How to make success possible.

...And so much more!

Sound too good to be true? It's not!

Karen has already inspired and guided HUNDREDS of authors and publishers towards success.

ARE YOU NEXT?

Table of CONTENTS

Introduction — 19	**Author Publisher Guide** — 23
4 Publishing Success Milestones — 77	**Top Tips** — 87
The Story — 107	**Your Story Journal** — 129

INTRODUCTION

EVERYONE HAS THE
ABILITY TO WRITE
AND PUBLISH A BOOK,
THEY JUST DON'T
KNOW IT YET...

IF you have purchased this book, then I will be bold and presume you are planning on publishing a book in the not too distant future.

Yes? Great. Let's get started.

In this guide you will learn how to get your book written, edited, published, marketed, and lots of other things that I have learnt along the way. When you enter this industry you will never be bored because the landscape is forever changing. There is always lots to do to learn, improve and move forward.

Since starting this journey I have been involved in more than 200 publishing projects that took anywhere from four weeks to twelve months to produce.
This book has come to be as a resource I can share with the world about how and why I do what I do.

Publishing can bring you places. If you are in business and you publish a book, it instantly raises your profile. If you are an aspiring author and you write and publish a book, you are one step closer to fulfilling that dream. If you aspire to share a message for the younger generation in a children's book, knowing how to navigate working with illustrators and how to set up your files etc are aspects that are within the capabilities of most of the population.

The secret ingredient is the desire to learn. I love to share my industry knowledge and secrets, so you will have all the tools you need to get your book published but what matters is what you do with this information. By reading this book you will be starting way ahead of me. I started with a seedling of an idea but not much knowledge and yet I am sharing everything you need to know in this book.

Publishing has changed and is no longer an unattainable dream. Yes, it is fabulous to be offered a contract with a big-name publisher who can place your book on every bookshop shelf, but in reality if you have not made waves in the literary scene beforehand, do not have a direct link inside the industry or a huge following, then the chance of that happening is limited.

So, I ask, why not become your own publisher?

Authors work increasingly hard to raise their profile to assist their publishers to sell books. Who do you think is going to make the most out of each book sale? The publisher of course! Rightly so, as they are the ones taking the financial risk on your book.

When you enter the publishing industry, the wealth of knowledge out there is amazing. In writing this book, it is my intention for you to gain enough knowledge and inspiration from my journey to apply it directly to successfully building your own publishing empire. There is enough room for us all in this world.

'When you are called to your purpose it comes naturally.'

AUTHOR-PUBLISHER GUIDE

What you need to know
to become a
successful author-publisher

PUBLISHING
noun

Publishing is the dissemination of literature, music, or information—the activity of making information available to the general public. In some cases, authors may be their own publishers, meaning originators and developers of content also provide media to deliver and display the content for the same.

why publish?

PUBLISHING TO GET YOUR WORK OUT THERE
If you have gone to the effort of writing your book and getting your words to be the best they can possibly be, then publishing is the next step. If securing a publishing deal with the 'big five' is off the cards then publishing yourself is an option. Whether you choose to do this with a company or independently, learning how to navigate the process is the key to success.

PUBLISH TO EARN IN INCOME
If you have an audience to sell your books to, and/or if you are in the process of building an author profile then you can earn more per book by publishing yourself and selling directly. Learning how to work this is in your best interest. When to offset your printing to meet distribution requirements is something we can all learn.

PUBLISH TO BUILD PROFILE/BRAND
The key strategy to publishing success is to build an author platform. That can be through your brand or as an author. Build your tribe from day one, it is this type of following that will get you on the best seller lists and on the radar of the big publishers. If you can sell books you will be appealing to more publishers.

Knowing how to navigate your publishing journey so that it aligns with your circumstances is important!

Use this page to write down your WHY for publishing, and what your hopes and aspirations are.

Your why is important as it will remain at the core of your motivation.

Why do you want to publish?

_____
_____
_____
_____
_____
_____
_____
_____
_____
_____
_____
_____
_____
_____
_____
_____
_____
_____
_____
_____

Building your Brand

Building your brand when do you start?

This subject is so important, especially if you want to sell books. Most big-name authors spend a lot of time building and promoting their brand to get in front of their readers and from there build a rapport with them. If you are in business, you may already have an established audience, so you are a step ahead.

Your brand is what people first experience when they interact with you (if you are the actual brand) or your business. Every experience, product, hearsay, interaction or anything associated with your brand has an impact on the empire you are creating. I was not always fully aware of this while building the Serenity Press brand. And yes, I made mistakes. However, I work hard to turn mistakes around in my favour. If you are aware of what to do from the start, then you are one step ahead already.

There will, of course, always be room to grow and expand your brand. But imagine if you got it right at the beginning of your journey.

Build your readership community from day one, they are your loyal tribe.

Here are some tips to consider:

Design: It makes a positive impact if your brand design is targeted toward the clientele you are hoping to attract. If design is not your strong point, then investing in this is definitely worth it. Think of it like a book cover. People are more likely to pick up and consider buying your book if they are attracted to it. Appealing to your niche is paramount at this stage.

Your logo is important. It benefits from being instantly identifiable and triggers a 'must have' emotional endorphin rush in your target consumer.

Mindfulness: People don't necessarily remember all details, but they will remember how they feel about certain books, products and services they have acquired. Focus some energy on ensuring you provide the emotional experience you hope to promote.

Every interaction you have, no matter how small, has the potential to build or damage your brand. Always aim for a best-case scenario.

Give more: I am a giving person by nature. I feel good when I give someone something they really desire. I have become a publisher because I love to give authors the dream of holding their book in their hands. I guide them through the often daunting process of publishing, and as you learn, you may consider doing the same. Karma is a wonderful thing in business.

Inspire: I have experienced firsthand the potential power words have in helping someone move forward, feeling supported and not alone. If you offer a service or product, give that little extra. It may make a big difference.

Helping others: Often the work I do out of the goodness of my heart leads to amazing affiliations, partnerships and sales, such as taking on community or charity projects. I do this with no expectation from the project other than to make something magical happen for those in need because this is important to me and makes my heart sing. Quite often the most amazing things find their way back to me through my act of kindness. It is important that if you choose to give, you do not expect to receive in return. Give with an open heart and the best of intention.

Integrity: Be that business people want to be part of; be the success story and defy odds. Be true to your values and principles as they are hard to retrieve once they are gone.

As you build your brand your business will evolve, your worth will increase and you will grow and bring more people or services on board. Grow at the organic speed of your business; don't push too hard, but be prepared to work hard when things are moving fast. It will all balance out. If your business keeps growing at a steady pace, it may be good to consider taking on a partner or some staff to help you out.

Plant seeds: Inspiration is a gift and, when pursued with passion, wonderful things can grow. Be brave, be innovative and be kind to yourself – it's going to be hard work.

Hard work and focus: People often admire others who work hard to achieve goals. Let's be honest, some people get lucky, but building, growing and sustaining a business is hard work and requires a lot of determination and focus. Nurture those seeds.

Partnerships: Partnering and affiliating with complementary brands and services is an amazing way to build your brand. When two businesses complement each other, clicking in place like jigsaw pieces, amazing things can happen for everyone involved. I love it when amazing people come together.

Treasure your tribe:

Since joining the Ausmumpreneur network, my opportunities have increased tenfold. Being a mother and building a business at the same time can be quite isolating and limiting, but in this fabulous community there are no obstacles to achieving everything you want for your business.

When I joined the network I had no expectations of making big sales or the amazing friendships and contacts I would establish. I am so proud that my hard-working and caring nature has been recognised and embraced wholly by this amazing group of women who lift each other up every day.

I advise you to find a strong network of like-minded people to help you move forward in your business. I was becoming a bit rigid until I did this. By surrounding myself with other successful businesses and businesswomen, I was introduced to the ways they 'made it'. I realised I wasn't fluffing my way through my business – I was actually doing well and if I implemented some structures and a more strategic business plan I would attract the type of financial backing I needed to be a successful business. I will talk more about this in a future chapter.

In summary, putting some time into building your brand from the beginning is important. Serenity Press has recently rebranded because we have changed towards a more traditional publishing model.

You can also build your own tribe of like-minded people whom you can inspire and grow alongside. It is wonderful to have cheerleaders!

Writing your Book

If you have not yet written your book this chapter is intended to inspire and guide you through the process.

I like to keep things simple and write from my heart. Recently I have also been incorporating my head in the process and the two make a winning combination. Now to find the time to do more of it ...

I will share possible ways to proceed successfully with these tasks, however it is important to note that many people find their own way to navigate their writing process. I hope you take something positive away from reading this.

Writing: The process

I have worked with many authors, and being an author myself, I have realised that taking shortcuts is often not the best practice. When I began writing, I was totally disillusioned about the process I have now come to respect wholeheartedly. I thought that when I wrote a book, that was the hard bit over! Sorry to burst the bubble, but it is just the beginning and that is why so many people don't make it. It was not necessarily a bad thing – sometimes ignorance is bliss. I liken it to having a baby (and I have had six). When you first get pregnant it is all romantic, but the pregnancy can be tough or smooth sailing ... and it takes time. The birth is painful, whether it is natural or surgical, but it is oh-so-worth-it when you hold that bundle of joy in your arms. And to think you would undertake it all again ...

There are plenty of people out there who can help you make your book the best it can be at a high price, but I feel it is important for the author to be more involved in how their book evolves.

If you want to do it right it is important to follow the process.

Think:

Get your thoughts down on paper and be creative. Your book wants you to write it. Write down everything you can think of and put it in some sort of order.

Jot down potential chapters, then scenes and characters for fiction (or content if you are writing self-help or non-fiction). I don't stress if what I am writing is not perfect. At this stage my focus is on getting down as much as I can. Research can be carried out during the preparation stage, but don't limit yourself to this, you may find that researching is a running theme throughout.

Writing your book is the action part of the process. You are getting words onto paper. It is not the time to worry, but to get writing and see where your story takes you. If you need to check something or come back to a scene, highlight a note in red within your document and return to it when you can.

Once you have your book written, what a great feeling it is. You want to celebrate and shout to the world: 'I have written a book! Here it is!' But it is important to be realistic and know that it is not ready to go out into the world quite yet. By all means, post the exciting news on social media that you have completed your first draft and share it with your loved ones. You deserve to celebrate as you have completed something that many people abandon.

The next steps are what will separate you from the amateurs. Do the hard work now and you will not regret it.

My advice is to put your book baby away for two weeks and revisit it with a clear mind. Then read it through and self-edit it as you go along, without being too harsh. When you have accomplished that stage you could ask a 'beta reader' to look over it for you. This could be another author or someone you respect who is willing to do this for you. Having a beta reader is always a great idea. They will want the best for your book and will invest their time and energy in providing feedback on content, flow and if they enjoyed your book. They will probably also create some anticipation for you on social media.

Perfectionism is wonderful but don't let it build a wall, blocking you from moving forward. This process is used by many successful authors, so don't be disheartened.

Consider the advice that your beta reader has provided, take on board what you know needs enhancing ... and then it is time to edit ...

The 5 step writing to publishing process:

1. Get your first draft out. (The Skeleton)
2. Second draft is a time to strengthen your book (The Muscle)
3. Your passion and mission are the heart and soul of your book, your book can't survive without them. (The Vital Organs)
4. The edit polishes your words and makes them beautiful. (The Skin) The proofread is the defining features.
5. The Cover design and typesetting (The Clothes)

My top editing tips are:

1. Go through your manuscript with different editing caps on.
2. Stay positive during the editing proces.
3. It's great to find a way that works for you.
4. Be proud – all of your hard work will pay off

Knowing that your book is the best it can be. will provide you with the confidence needed to promote it and see it become a best seller with an abundance of five-star reviews.

Editing is so important and published books are edited many times before they make it to the shelves.

And let's not forget the final important step... The proofread!

A proofread is different than an edit as it makes sure that there are no spelling errors and design is consistent and commas are in the right place.

Importance of editing

Editing is one of the most important aspects of completing your book. It can also be one of the most tedious stages. The level of editing required will depend on your writing skills. Even if you feel that you are not a good editor, I advise you to go over your manuscript at least twice. Firstly, as a reader to check the flow of your book. Secondly, to correct any typos and grammatical issues.

Working through those stages is wonderful and makes your manuscript stronger. Again, sorry to be the bearer of bad news, but this does not necessarily mean your manuscript is ready to go to print.

It is important that you make your work the best it can be, so at this stage you can outsource to an editor. There are some amazing editors in my publishing academy who are trustworthy and will provide you with an honest assessment of your manuscript.

If you only plan to write one book, you might not feel the need to upskill your editing skills, however if you do intend to write more books it is a worthwhile investment. Many of us feel time poor in this busy business world, but my advice is not to cut corners on editing.

The different types of editing include:
1. DEVELOPMENTAL EDIT (Intensive)
2. STRUCTUARL EDIT
3. COPYEDIT
4. PROOFREAD

Below is a diagram from grammarfactory.com

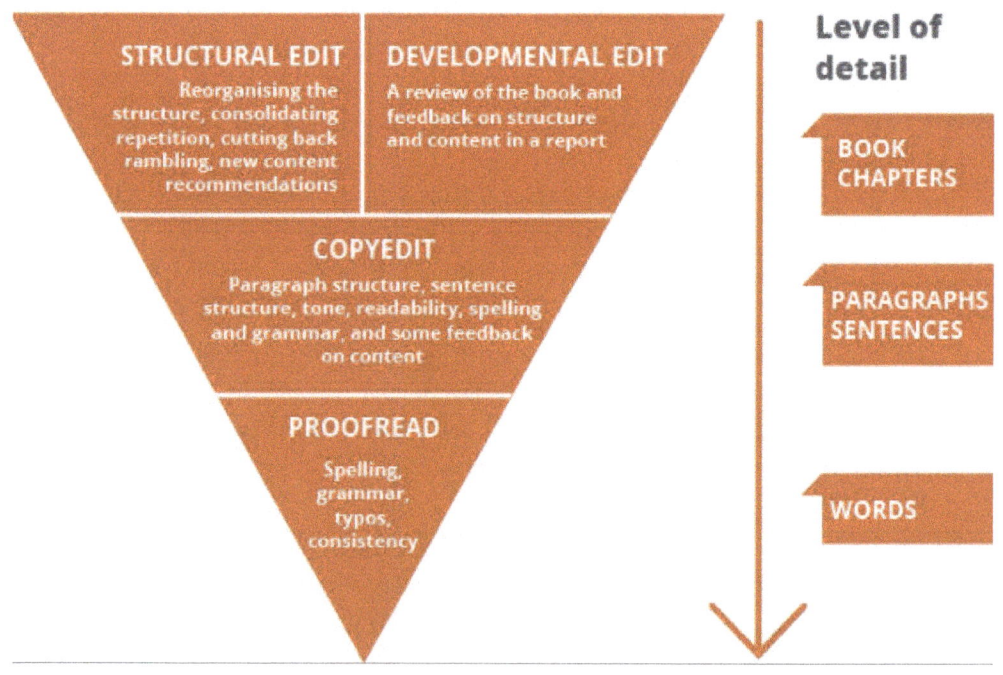

Publishing your book

The landscape of publishing has certainly changed over the past 5 - 10 years. Many authors have altered their perspective on how traditional publishing is perceived. Self-publishing is no longer frowned upon as it once was. There are now many self-published authors consciously choosing to be in control, and by connecting with their inner entrepreneur they are doing really well. This is great news for aspiring authors. You no longer need to sit around hoping that a traditional publisher will send you a publishing offer rather than a rejection. You can take positive action towards publishing your own book. This is an ideal scenario for action-based entrepreneurs.

A little about my journey

When I began writing, I aspired to be a successful author. I self-published my first novel with a vanity press. It was a negative experience, however through that experience I learnt the process of publishing a book. Time and circumstance aligned and I was ready to act when opportunity arose and so my journey has continued to where I find myself today. My inner entrepreneur didn't feel happy clinging onto a small hope that my book might be 'picked up' by a publisher. I chose to take positive action to work towards my dream. I knew it may take time to perfect but I was open and excited to learn new things. In doing so I could also help others publish their books in a positive way and collect stories for inspiring anthologies. If I can do it, so can you.

I am going to chat about three options for you as an author:

1. Self-published author.
2. Traditionally published author.
3. Author-publisher.

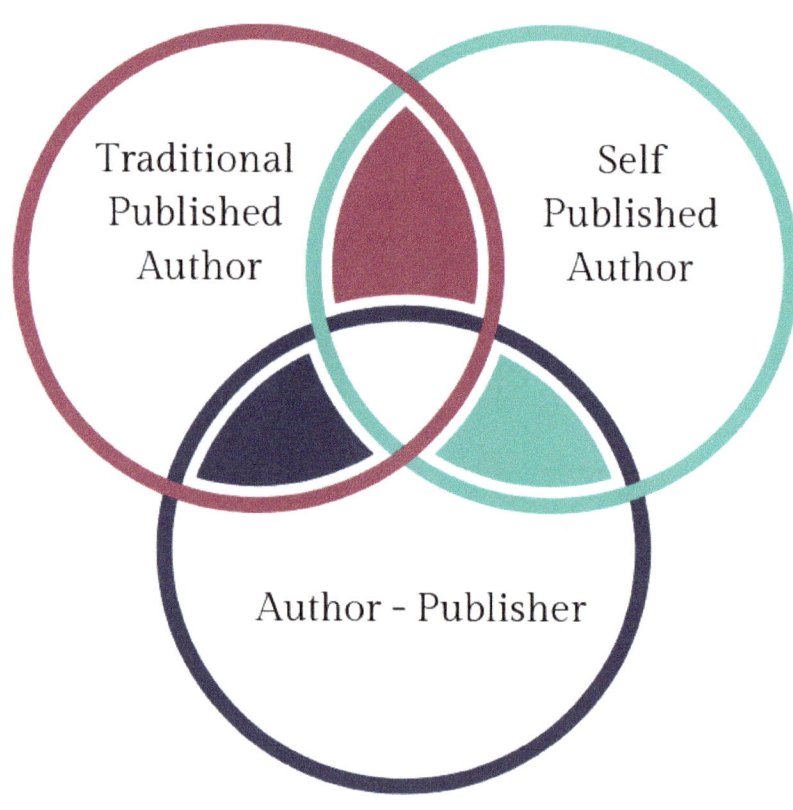

Self-Publishing

You have written a book and chosen to self-publish it. What do you do?

As a self-publishing author it is up to you to make sure your book is as good as it can be. It's all well and good to write a book and publish it, but ensuring the quality is equal to that of a traditionally published book is the key to making your book saleable. I highly recommend self-editing and if you can afford it, professional editing, or at least a proofread.

There are many platforms you can use to publish your book. KDP (Kindle Direct Publishing, owned by Amazon) and IngramSpark (owned by Ingram Content Group) are two of the most popular. Through these platforms your book will be available worldwide in print and eBook formats. You will need to have your files prepared and ready for uploading in pdf format for print and epub for eBook. Both platforms have plenty of guidance on how to publish with them so it is worthwhile taking some time to learn. It is a cost effective way to publish your book and reach your readership.

You will discover that setup fees are quite similar no matter whether you have a 400-page novel or a 22-page children's book. KDP is very popular with authors because there is no charge for revisions and everything is quite automatic. They have a template you can load into and lots of advice on how to make your book visually appealing.

Living in Australia, I suggest you consider Ingram-Spark as they have an office and printing house in Melbourne. They print black and white and colour books through there and you can have them quite fast if need be, and even pick them up yourself if you are Melbourne-based. Ingram also has printing house partners in the UK and America. There is also an option to rush both production and shipping. This option is priceless when you have a deadline, but it is important to remember that it does cost extra. If you need a colour print run it is commissioned through their US printing house. They do not charge you the extra shipping costs, but it will take at least three weeks to receive your order so plan well ahead.

We used the Lightning Source division of Ingram for our print-on-demand (POD) titles when we started out. We moved to Ingram Spark as they began to overtake Lightning Source on many different levels and the prestigiousness of publishing through them did not hold the value it first did.

I suggest you create an account with Ingram Spark if you aspire to having your own publishing press. They are recognised by bookstores, which is important when you are in the business.

All in all, you can publish your book quite inexpensively yourself and have it available globally through online retailers. If you would only like to have your book available as a Kindle eBook, you can do this by creating an account through KDP Select. My advice is to upload your manuscript in Word format as it will transfer better. For children's books, I suggest you download the Kindle Kids Book Creator. You can upload your pdf file and it will be transformed into a .mobi file, perfect for Kindle.

There are numerous self-publishing businesses ready to publish your book straight away. There are costs involved, all differing depending on the level of service you require. You really can do it yourself but if it is overwhelming or you don't have the time or computer skills required, it is advantageous to source assistance.

- Do your homework to find the right assistance for you
- Costs can vary considerably so be mindful who you choose.

Traditional publishing

Having a big-name publisher take on your book is a dream scenario for many authors. You will not have the control or commission from each sale that self-publishing offers, but you will have an established market ready to buy your book.

If you approach a publisher and they reject your manuscript, it is important to remember it is not always a reflection of the quality of your work. It could be a case of your book not fitting with their publishing schedule at that time, or your book could be similar to another that has already been accepted. There are a number of people at a publishing house involved in the decision about whether to take on a new title. Sometimes a manuscript will go to an acquisitions meeting, but the publisher cannot convince the sales and marketing team to say yes. The best way to secure a publisher is through a literary agent who will know what each publisher is looking for at any given time. However it is not an easy feat to secure an agent.

One way to draw attention to yourself is to demonstrate how well you will sell your books, and this means getting yourself 'out there'. If you have a big online following, you should have a better chance of securing a deal with a publisher.

It is worth noting that you will receive a smaller percentage of sales, however your workload will be greatly reduced if your book is traditionally published opposed to self-publishing.

There are many advantages to publishing a book, especially if it complements your business or fits in with a popular genre. You will also gain instant credibility as many people aspire to become an author, often perceiving it to be an unachievable goal. Attracting the attention of the media is more successful when you are an author.

The purpose of this book is for you to consider becoming your own publisher and whether the benefits of self-publishing outweigh those of being with one of the 'big five' publishers.

Author-Publisher

So, what is an author-publisher?

My definition is: *An author who builds a platform where they will seek to obtain contracts with traditional publishers but will also have in place a publishing team that they will utilise to publish the books they wish to represent themselves.*

It means that less books are left at the bottom of a pile.

Being a traditionally published author and remaining under contract is hard work. It doesn't suit every author, especially those who want to explore different styles of writing. I might even go so far as to say that it is the lucky ones who get to transition through the seasons of their writing journey.

Being an author-publisher is ideal for authors who write well, are building a readership and who want to be in control of their own author journey and/or leverage their readership to make the most of launch sales.

Being an author-publisher gifts you the freedom to write the book that calls the loudest and then see if it is of interest to your publisher. If not it is not the end of the world as you will go through the process of publishing yourself and bring your book out your way, because you can.

It is OK for publishers to say no, publishers can only take on board the books they have planned to focus on.

It would take a very special book or author to make a publisher steer off track.

There will be times when that doesn't align. But that does not need to mean failure, nor does it have to mean waiting a year or two for another publisher to pick up.that manuscript.

The way the publishing industry is now, it means that you:
- get a cover designed
- have your book edited
- proofread
- typeset
- promoted
- published
- distributed
- promoted some more.

The authors who embrace being an author-publisher fuse tradional publishing and self-publishing.

AUTHOR-PUBLISHER

SUCCESS TEAM

YOU

EDITOR & PROOFREADER

DESIGNER

DISTRIBUTOR

PR / MARKETING

RIGHTS MANAGEMENT

ELECTRONIC eBooks

eBooks can be used to your advantage while publishing a book. In fact, some eBook publishers focus solely on eBook distribution which cuts out significant production costs, however it doesn't cut out editing.

Direct book sales are where you will make the most per book income. However there are a lot of customers out there with ready access to their electronic reading devices who can access your book instantly when they come across it, are in contact with you or if you are recommended to them. Readers who love their electronic reading device will rarely buy a print copy unless it is at an author event and they can get it signed.

Another thing to keep in mind is to keep your title at a reasonable price. You won't make bestseller status by having your eBook listed for $9.99 if you are largely unknown. Best-selling novelists will get away with this on the book's release as demand is high and readers are willing to invest in the writer. If that is not the case for you I would suggest modest pricing for your eBook.

Amazon has an option to check the recommended pricing for your type of book so I suggest utilising that if you are going with KDP (Kindle Direct Publishing) . Your book should be approved overnight with KDP.

While Amazon is a major eBook distributer, they are not the only company offering this service. Kobo, Nook and iTunes also sell eBooks. IngramSpark have a good low-cost eBook distribution service. One file set up and your title is distributed to the major eBook sellers, so it is definitely worth considering clicking 'convert to ebook' when your book files have been set up. It takes 14 days to transfer.

eBook success

eBooks are a great way to leverage reaching best seller status.

In the instance of Amazon best seller you can use a proven strategy to hit number one on your eBook launch day.

- Did you know that Amazon update sales every two hours for their top 100 in each category?
- Did you know that it can take less than 100 eBook sales in one focused hour or across one focused day that will get you to number one in your category?
- Did you know that being strategic with some of your categories is a bonus?

For NYT (New York Times) best seller list sales need to be on release week and through American eBook distributors like Amazon etc.

* I recommend that you set your ebook launch at least a fortnight after your actual release date.

DISTRIBUTE
Selling Books

You have published your book and now want to get it into the hands of every possible reader. How do you do it?

I have learnt so much about selling books since focusing my intention on distribution.

There are many ways of selling your book. The diagram below displays available options

Through POD (Print on Demand), eBooks, direct to customer, bulk orders and wholesale distribution.

POD (Print on demand)

POD is a fabulous way to publish your book with minimal financial commitment and risk. If you have an established readership, you are one major step ahead and I would suggest a more commercial approach to sales. However POD still will have its place in servicing global customers.

With POD you can have your book available through worldwide distribution. This means your files will be available to print in printing houses situated in different locations across the globe to service your readers internationally. Customers will be able to source your title through a leading online book store; the order will be processed without you having to do a thing. Alternatively, a customer may order a book through you and you can process it on your account with your printing/distribution company (Ingram Spark, Lightning Source).

Shipping orders internationally from Australia can be costly, so it is cheaper to set up files through these distribution channels even if you have printed a bulk order to be stored in your warehouse I would still recommend this option for overseas orders. (However, specialised printing is limited).

POD is also a really productive way to get your book published and then pursue media attention, distributors etc. Once they have a tangible product in their hands it is easier for them to say yes than if they just have a concept.

Catalogues

It is beneficial to have your book displayed in catalogues alongside other books in your genre, whether direct to the customer or a book buyer. There are many different catalogues out there so find where your title fits and try to have it included.

Schools and Libraries

Libraries and schools buy a lot of books. Each state will have its own sales direct representative for schools and libraries. In Western Australia it is Westbooks. The key is to liaise with them and arrange an appointment. Have your book catalogued with the National Library of Australia with an ISBN and have a copy of your book stocked there. James Bennett is also a direct library supplier and they have a link to Booktopia.

Bookstores

To see your book stocked on a bookshelf is something very special for every author; it is the ultimate dream. This is possible for self-published authors but is unlikely unless you have a big following or a distribution company. You will need to think and invest like a publishing house to make it happen. It is important to remember that you will be the one taking the financial risk, not the retailer.

Here is an example of how you can make it happen.

Firstly, it is advised that you reduce the cost of your book production to enable to you to make a profit. Working with distributors and bookstores can really eat into your profits, which allows the bookstore leverage for a competitive price on your title while making money themselves.

Many direct to store distributors are closed to individual accounts, however it is still worth asking. Novella Distribution is a new distributor who is active in getting books out to stores, into schools and distributed generally. They tell you how many books they expect to sell, you send them to them on consignment and receive a monthly record of sales.

Another option is to research sales representatives who introduce books in your genre to stores. When you approach them it is advisable to have a strong pitch explaining why they should add your book to their schedule.

Titlepage is a database where bookstores in Australia and New Zealand often go to source titles in specific genres. The key to capitalising here is to have your book categorised correctly. If you are confused contact them, they are very happy to help.

Working with bookstores individually in your local area is fine but it takes a lot of time. They want a high percentage of profits, often up to 45 per cent of recommended retail price (RRP) and distributors will want more than that, often up to 70 percent.

You will also be requested to place books there on consignment and chasing payments is never a nice thing to do. In my experience and in feedback from authors who have pursued this path, it has always ended up being a costly time-consuming venture. This is not to say that with the right focus and contacts you won't be successful in supplying directly to individual stores.

It is my hope that you channel your time and energy to the most productive sales channel for your book.

eBook distribution

The main eBook sellers are Amazon Kindle, Barnes & Noble and iBooks. You can set up files directly to each of these platforms or utilise your account through Ingram Spark, who service all three retailers. They do require that you have your files in epub format.

Amazon Kindle's KDP platform is easy to manage. The format to upload to this platform is Word and for your children's books you can use their Kindle Kids Book Creator as it turns your files easily into .mobi files. It is easy to manage offers and there is a helpful price setting section in the setup process. Sales are easy to monitor on your account also, so you can gauge what campaigns are most effective.

The key to achieving sales in eBooks is to have your book not too highly priced, have effective keywords in place and encourage readers to review your book. Be pro-active in promoting your eBook. There are lots of eBook readers in the world and you need to make your eBook stand out from the crowd so that readers will press the buy button.

You can now set your eBook up on pre-order for pre-sales in anticipation of a launch, and it will be delivered to your customer's reading device on release day.

Best seller status is highly achievable with eBooks. This often happens through a promotional discount period and when partnered with influencers in your genre or a widely anticipated launch. It is important that your book is categorised for success so take some time in placing it in the right category during setup.

The cover is a major selling point so if you are not a

savvy cover designer it is best to hire a professional as it is important to make your book visually appealing to your customer.

Give to receive

When you are marketing your book in anticipation of its launch it is most definitely worth compiling a list of influencers to receive gifts of your book. In the publishing world these books are called Advanced Reading Copies (ARCs) and are important to stimulate interest before release. Connect with these influencers and try to have them agree to read your book before you send it. If the right person promotes your book at the right time, magic happens.

Many of our individual sales waves come when someone with a strong social media presence promotes your book through a review.

Bulk sales

We are all big thinkers here so let's start thinking bulk orders and have a more commercial mindset.

If you have a big social media following or a very strong partnership with an influencer who is willing to promote your book, focusing energy into a big pre-order campaign is the way to go. This way you will secure enough sales to make bulk print viable and you cut out the middle men in the process. The reality is that there is a lot of work in processing orders so that is something to be mindful of.

Focusing energy in targeting a bulk order from a business that is interested in your genre of book is also a very smart move. I have seen many authors successfully secure contracts to supply bulk orders for their titles. Again, you would mould your pitch to suit the business you are approaching.

Bulk sales are a great way to achieving Best Selling order status. This is a great accolade to have when hosting events and public speaking appearances, which in turn are also great opportunities to capitalise on sales. Readers love to meet the author and have their book personally signed, or alternatively you could have them pre-signed for sales throughout the event without having to be there.

This leads me onto the option of a book tour. If your book is commercial enough it is worth considering a book tour. This can be a costly exercise and often authors team up and visit a few major cities where readers will come to meet and greet. It is also an investment in yourself if you are hoping to publish future books and create a following. Readers love to know their author.

Commercial distribution

Finding the right distributor can be challenging but it is not impossible. Distributors want to sell books – that's how they make an income. Get yourself best prepared to be accepted by having a strong marketing campaign in place. Ensure your book is the best quality you can at minimal cost to you, ensuring that you can capitalise on this. Think like a publisher!

It is important to note that return per book is not much when supplying to distributors, sometimes as low as 30 per cent of RRP. But the capacity to sell books is dramatically increased so it is up to you to determine if you are prepared to take a risk.

Woodslane is an approachable distribution company

based in Sydney. You can register with them and have your book stocked in their warehouse if they take you on. You can stock 100 copies or 1000, depending on how big your marketing campaign will be. I talked with an inside contact who informed me that you can expect to typically sell 200 books with a small marketing campaign and 1200 or more with a national campaign. It is also good to know they have Big W on their portfolio.

New South books are another big distributor for publishing houses, but are closed to taking on new accounts at present. Their distribution house is TPL Distribution so it may be worth pursuing an account with them.

There are lots of different ways to sell your book. Take some time to sit down and work out exactly what is the right blend for your book.

A few tips to sales success:
- Do your research
- Undertake relevant marketing, marketing and more marketing;
- Find out who the big publishing houses use to distribute in your genre and contact them directly;
- Pursue the big sales opportunities – that can be a single wave of sales or bulk sales;
- Build your brand.

I do wish for high sales volumes for us all. We all have so much to share with each other and a book filled with priceless, precious information is a minimal investment with high potential for each reader. This should not be under-valued; it should be treasured.

There is enough room for multiple best-selling books in this world so let's not compete with each other. I suggest we elevate each other. Some of the best-selling romance authors I know all support each other; they have an amazing tribe of followers who are keen to discover a new amazing talent.

This year I am delighted to be a part of the Small Press Network (SPN) distribution subcommittee. This proactive group of small publishers have banded together to make a positive difference in getting books onto store shelves and increasing sales for the smaller publishers. Watch this space.

Marketing basics

Knowing how to market your book is really important in creating a hype about an impending release. You can take advantage of pre-sales and your book will hopefully fly off the shelves on release.

I have heard that it takes someone to see something seven times before it leaves an imprint on their memory. Logically, this makes complete sense and indicates that you should have your book displayed everywhere your target audience may be.

Market a book well and watch as it takes off. It doesn't have to cost a fortune, however adopting strategic planning is important.

A marketing plan should be specific for each book although the most important core principles of marketing can be the same and enhanced accordingly.

The following is an example of how we marketed a romance anthology featuring six authors that we launched in November 2015.

The book was set in our hometown and we wanted to get people talking about it because of its local setting. We made the front page of one of the local papers!

Business of Publishing

Building your business – partnerships,
business knowledge – memberships

If you hope your publishing business will grow, regardless of whether you are just publishing your own books or have taken the plunge to publish or represent others, it is important to be part of a community of supportive business individuals who will inspire you to think bigger and take informed risks.

What do you believe?

I was recently a panellist at the Women's Business School in Perth, which was hosted by the amazing Peace and Katy from Ausmumpreneur. They invited me to join them for the whole day and it was an amazing experience. We worked through lots of amazing business enhancing exercises and I learnt lots. I was challenged outside my comfort zone in a safe way and it worked wonders. I left feeling so excited about the new directions Serenity Press is taking, and even though I am taking on some huge projects I am excited about each of them. This is largely because of the support, encouragement and knowledge I receive from the Ausmumpreneur network. Thinking big isn't as frightening as it could potentially have been.

When business is broken down into small steps it doesn't seem such a huge endeavour.

During the day we were asked to partner with someone to share our three Whys. These are the essence of what we believe in and gift us with our heart-centred goal for our business. Our passion, our drive and our enthusiasm comes from these core beliefs so this exercise is simple, yet very powerful when embraced whole-heartedly.

> My three beliefs are:
> 1. I believe we all can make magic happen.
> 2. I believe we all can have a positive impact on each other's lives.
> 3. I believe in the power of the written word.

When the third belief flowed through me and out of my mouth it came with such intensity that my partner went 'Wow'. I knew she felt the energy that was emitted with each word. So when everyone was asked to share their beliefs – and with a little nudge in my back from my partner – I said, 'I believe in the power of the written word.' Again, gasps – these words that came straight from my heart-centred core were having the impact I had hoped for.

It was through writing my first book The Visitor that I learnt how effective writing with this energy is. Every word in that book was penned through the same heart-centred intensity. I have had many people connect with me saying they don't know exactly why, but the book had reached into their hearts and given them the answer they longed for.

I know without a shadow of a doubt that it is the same energy I founded Serenity Press with. Every endeavour I pursue using this magic attracts the most beautiful people my way. Unexpected things happen and everything falls into place just as it should be. It is a very fulfilling feeling to know the business you created through your heart-centred goal, with not much more than the knowing feeling you were doing the right thing, is embraced by the people you hoped to embrace.

Serenity Press has turned the page and started a new chapter. Amazing things are happening in a big way, with an amazing heart-centred team supporting us. We are grateful, we are ambitious and we are excited about how the future is shaping for our press. We are here for the long haul, with strong foundations in place that we are hard at work building upon to create a legacy of books to be proud of.

All of this has been possible because of unwavering belief. I believe, and through the actions I have taken through that belief, others believe too.

And through that belief you can grow. Serenity Press grew and because of that MMH Press, Karen Mc Dermott Brand and the Everything Publsihing Academy we're born.

Through embracing evolution growth is inevitable. By growing my publishing press, building my team and in turn finding time to write my books I am also aligning myself for success as an author because I will be well connected and able to position myself for success when the time and circumstance align. Only I an know when that time is right.

What are your three core beliefs?

My 3 core beliefs are

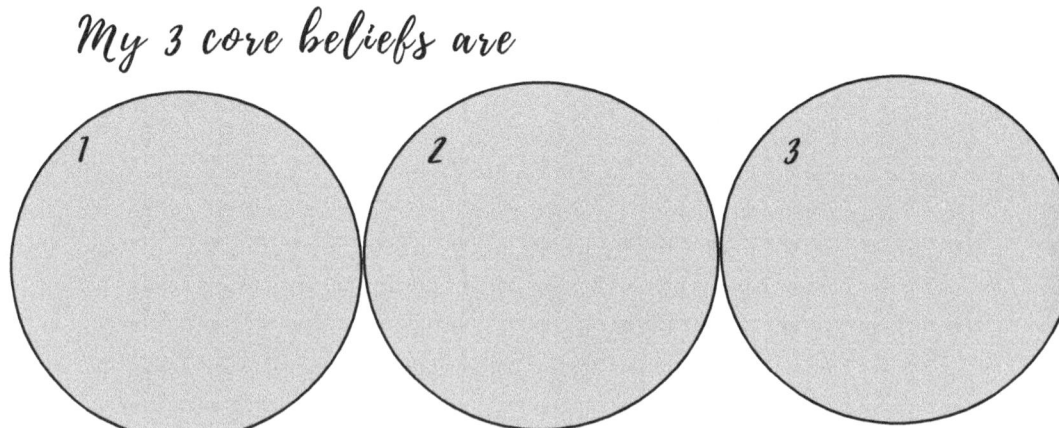

Heart-writing for business

I discovered early on that writing articles is a wonderful way of building a relationship with clients and people interested in what you have to offer. Putting a lot of information on a page may leave someone informed but have you given the best of you? Have you truly engaged and connected with them?

The articles I write through heart writing are the ones that get the most positive comments and are read more widely. Why? Because it is obvious that I am authentic and willing to share myself with my readers, therefore I connect on a deeper level.

This type of connection is important as it is like a tattoo imprinting into your reader's heart and mind. They will be willing to invest in what you have to offer if they feel a connection. They will remember how you made them feel and therefore they may seek other articles you have written which may lead them to books, workshops and services that you may have on offer. This is the highest form of engagement when building your profile. People will want to remember you and talk about you to their friends and groups.

People will always remember how you made them feel.

I have watched many people build their profiles through heart writing. It is a positive if you are resilient and only focus on what your intention may be. It is important to be mindful that you are not going to please everyone.

When you engage the right person/audience, then your platform will expand, and before you know it you will have a wider audience than ever before. It is your job to ensure you are ready for that to happen. When sudden growth takes place it can be really overwhelming if you are not prepared for it, so always think big. (I will chat about that in another article).

I believe in the power of the written word. This is one of my core beliefs. I am truly passionate about it and when I write I open my heart; the words just flow out. My first novel was written directly through this channel and it still conjures up all kinds of emotions in people. The connections I am proudest of are the ones where, through my words, people found comfort in their time of grief. Others have found hope and others heard words of wisdom. All readers vary.

For a number of years, I wrote for a website called Building Beautiful Bonds. It was at a time when I was experiencing huge personal growth. My articles were read more than 56,000 times so I knew that I was engaging with people. We did not promote the site or articles at all so this was a triumph. I have compiled the main articles into a book I called Heart Writer.

It is now deemed a strength to share your challenges. It gives your profile more depth. There is no need to hide behind a screen. Stepping out and sharing your 'why' is a very powerful way to attract people to your business. I regularly share my experiences and people who take the time to connect with me discover that I am a very passionate, driven person who has a heart-centred passion for everything she endeavours.

So the next time you are writing an article or sharing your business story, consider putting some heart into it. It could end up being one of your best investments.

Blogging

Blogging is a good way to build an audience and build your brand. Your readers will get to know you and a relationship of trust will already have been established. Your readers will also be familiar with your style of writing and won't think twice about investing in your book.

Blogging does take time and commitment though. Readers will want to read something from you pretty regularly and you should aim for at least one blog a week to build momentum.

Here are some ideas that successful authors use:

- have giveaways of other authors' books.

- showcase other authors by interviewing them.

- share your writing and publishing journey.

- be giving and generous in your energy. (Help your readers fall in love with you even more.)

- reviews other authors' books. (This is really good for appearing in front of huge audiences.)

You can connect a blog to your website which will drive traffic through your point of sale. That is always a good thing, especially if your website is visually appealing to your niche market.

Name of your blog

Website

Having a website is not compulsory these days as a lot of activity happens on social media platforms.

However, it is advised to have a visually appealing website as a go-to for readers to have a hub filled with info about you and/or your publishing press.

Why?

It is a one-stop platform solely dedicated to your authorship/publishing press, that holds all of your important information in one place without potential clients having to scroll through news feeds.

Imagine if you lost a huge opportunity because you didn't have a website.

Pages to consider when setting up your website:

- Inviting home page. (Project your brand theme.)
- Author page. (Informative with Q&A, interviews, video, call-to-action for newsletter.)
- Publications list. (Book cover(s), reviews, awards, purchase link.)
- Blog
- Contact page. (I recommend email or a contact me form.)

These five elements are important when designing a website. There are many other pages that you can add such as a media page for journalists to source details about you.

When building your website you can use a free website platform: Wordpress and Wix both have free options. I use Wix as it is easier to navigate and the styles are modern. It is also safe from viruses. With both options you can buy a domain relatively inexpensively. We have a store that has the added protection of PayPal so I know my customers are safe.

If the prospect of building a website is terrifying for you I suggest you hire someone. If going with Wix I recommend using one of their experts as they are knowledgeable and inexpensive.

I recall when I knew nothing about websites and a company who built the website I wrote for was commissioned to add one page designated to my new venture. They charged $750 for 20 hours' work and the page I was left with was really basic and practically unusable. In 2012 that was alot of money and I know now for what was done it was way too expensive.

I have since discovered the platform I use now where for just over $200 a year I have my own domain, store and heaps of add-on apps that I can use and update easily. It is also easy to build and learn how to navigate.

Your website represents you, so dress it well and make sure it says what you want it to say.

Illustrators

If you are publishing a children's book or a book that includes illustrations, it is important to build a relationship with your illustrator. You will be working closely with them, which at times may require pushing boundaries. Mutual respect for each other will help you overcome hurdles if they arise.

When you find an illustrator who draws in the style you like, does the work within the timeframe and is easy to get along with, cherish them, they are worth treasuring. Let them know how much you value them and how grateful you are.

There is a process to illustrating a vision. Below is an example of how My Silly Mum came to be.

It is hard work but so worth it when you see it all develop into something worthy of commercial distribution.

Talks and event bookings

As you become increasingly more established as an author or publisher you may be invited to do a talk or deliver a workshop. This is a great opportunity to sell books and usually you will get paid. There will be instances when you won't. It is up to you if you pursue them or not. I do as many as possible as it is free marketing for my business and an opportunity for me to build my profile while doing something good.

Another option you may consider is creating your own event specific to your area of expertise. My advice is to see through your first event without much expectation, ensuring that you give it your all. This should result in a positive outcome with word of mouth to follow.

Recommendations from others in important circles is imperative to achieve success through events. You will then be able to promote in these circles successfully for future workshops. Keep moving forward and if you discover a winning workshop along the way, stick it out.

Awards, reviews and best seller status

Becoming an award-winning author or business will assist you in increasing your brand profile. Accolades like these help others sit up and take notice of your work. It is important to share these achievements as you gain them, it helps maintain momentum alongside your writing journey.

It was through being a finalist in the Ausmumpreneur awards in 2015 that I raised the profile of Serenity Press. A buzz surrounded me and helped me to stand out from the crowd. I embraced the momentum and ran with it. It has been like a snowball running down a hill, continuously growing and gaining momentum. Take time to enter awards that are relevant to you. Be prepared to invest in yourself. Let's face it, being an author is being a small business.

In 2016 I won the Ausmumpreneur award because I thought big and in doing so won big. I hired an Irish castle which raised the vibration of Serenity Press and attracted more established authors our way which would help us in raising the profile of our brand so that out emerging authors would benefit.

Reviews by influencers i.e. fellow authors, friends, celebrities and influencers to your target audience can make a real difference when promoting a book. Reviews are a sure-fire way to get readers interested in your book. I have witnessed many successes because the right person fell in love with an author's book. It is your job, as the author or publisher, to ensure the book is readily available so that when a wave in sales occurs you are ready to capitalise on it. Such success can also lead to best seller status.

This can be achieved in a few different ways. Through eBook sales via Amazon, selling books in stores and directly. Authors often have a promotion leading up to release day. This is a great opportunity to gain eBook sales that can lead to being number one in your chosen category during release week. There is also that added option of having an eBook pre-order which in turn helps with the spike in sales on release day. Being in Australia helps as Amazon has a designated Kindle site and so sales are gauged on Australian sales and if you have an Australian readership you could be onto a winner.

Pursuing awards, reviews and best-selling status can be time consuming, but the rewards are ten-fold when it comes together.

Readers Favorite is a review and award company that I believe every author-publisher should connect with. My first book received a huge five-star review and went on to become a finalist in their 2012 book awards contest. I was invited to Miami for their awards ceremony which is held during Miami Book Fair every year.

Social media

Having a social media presence is a must for authors wanting to build a profile. My online presence is very strong. Even if it doesn't reflect on the normal everyday reality of my life, it does showcase my business journey. In turn I have built a network of amazing people who feel that they are part of my journey too, and they are, as they are cheering from the sidelines.

Facebook is a fabulous place to be present when you are in business and an author. I have a rule wherein I block out all negatives and only focus on positives and it works. There are lots of negative people on there but when you adopt this rule from day one, navigating Facebook is a more productive experience. You will need to have a profile and from that an author/business page where you accumulate likes. You can run promotions and showcase on other people's pages to gain likes. Often success is measured by how many likers you have. Many successful businesses have been built upon this platform.

Twitter is not as personal as Facebook and anonymity is more achievable through this platform. It has evolved to be more about business. I have had success through tagging in celebrities and media via Twitter. The key is to have an eye-catching image or headline so that your tweet stands out. Be mindful that your tweet will be seen by many people who know your brand so keep within the perimeters of your brand integrity.

Instagram has fast become one of the best ways to build a profile. Images talk volumes on this platform. Have a good camera and develop an eye for detail when sharing images. It is a great marketing tool and gaining followers is faster than on Twitter and Facebook.

All-in-all, social media is the way to go if you want to create a genuine following. It is also a wonderful way to reflect back on your journey to success.

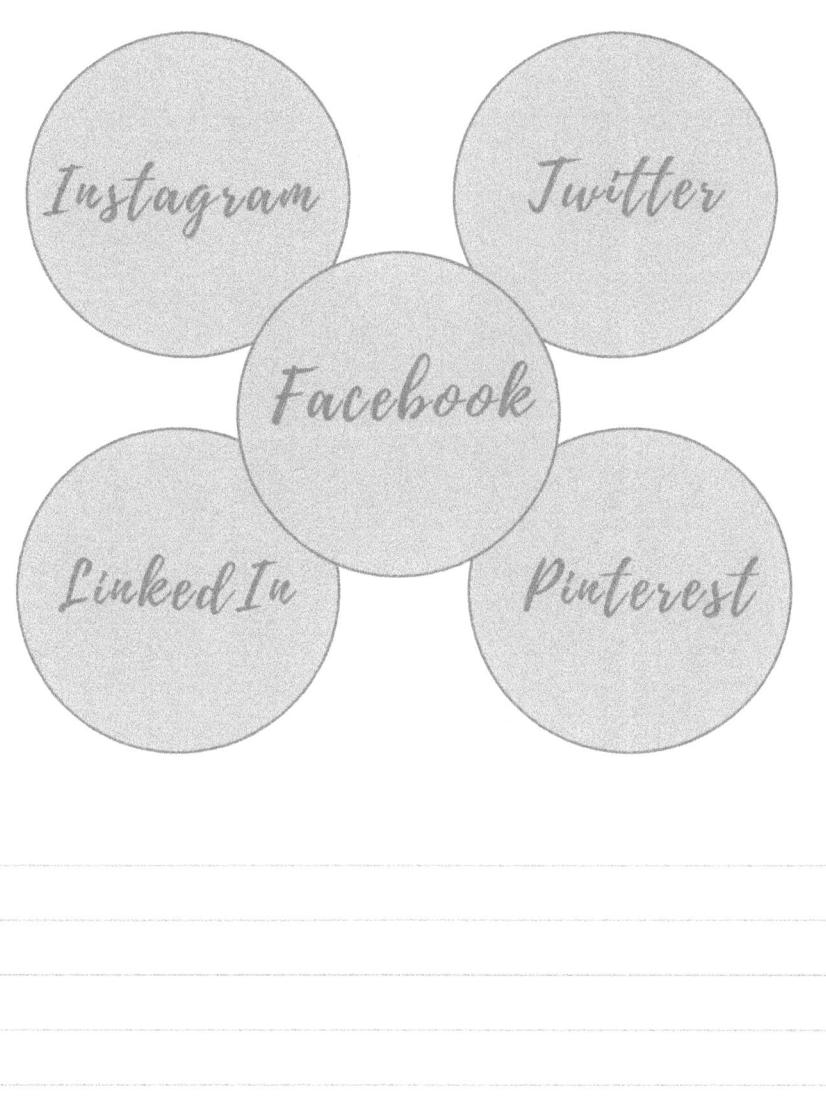

Build your database

Your database is your direct line of contact to potential customers and well worth the effort to compile.

An effective way to build a database is through a newsletter pop up – you know, those annoying things that pop up when you visit a website?

Collect email addresses like gold coins. Each one is worth more.

Regular Newsletters

Giveaways

Collaborations

Pop up on website to capture visitors

List swaps

Show up consistently

MINDSET
Think like a publisher

Financials

Keeping on top of your finances is imperative if you are to be a successful business. That doesn't mean you have to penny pinch, on the contrary it assists in helping you to invest in your business the right way.

I have learnt this the hard way. For the first few years of business I just collected a pile of receipts in a box and on my computer and when tax time came around I was drowning in a pile of paper.

That is my past and now I have implemented spreadsheets that track income and expenditure. It is very liberating as a business to know where you stand financially. Until I got to this point I felt like I had more of an expensive hobby than a business but now I know that my business has great value.

Quickbooks is an inexpensive resource to use for managing your daily accounts. It even syncs with PayPal and our bank so that everything can be managed together. This is good for my business as a large percentage of our online sales go through PayPal. There are also other resources that come highly recommended by many businesses, including Xero and MYOB. You can also keep your own spreadsheets and your accountant can assist you in managing them.

As you grow it is important to have a structure in place so that you don't have to worry about organising finances and will have financial data at the touch of a button if need be. This is an ideal and a real possibility if you focus energy on building a strong foundation early on.

There are so many other financial considerations, such as funding your business, grants, investing and many other elements. These opportunities will be specific to your business journey. It is important to find a strategy that works for your business, just like I did for mine.

Being confident about your financial position is the key to success. The main goal of business is to be profitable so that should be the key focus.

One key thing I remember hearing on my journey that has stuck with me is that businesses do not run out of cashflow, the owners run out of the passion to find creative ways to create cashflow for their growing business.

Set the intention of what you want to achieve. Know that you will need to invest to increase the value of your author-publisher ventures but that by strategically positioning yourself in front of your readers you are aligning yourself with a high level of success in your future. It takes courage but when you connect with your channel of Knowing, then you will be able to make unwavering decisions without fear.

One of my life mantras has always been:

Where there is a will, there is always a way.

Having a positive mindset that takes action will see you reach the highest heights.

There are key components that will serve you well in your pursuit of author-publisher success.

Courage- It takes courage to be an author-publisher. Quite often you will be treading on unfamiliar ground and so it is imperative to be guided by instinct and remain connected with your knowing.

Curiosity – This keeps things interesting! Being curious is a natural instinct to pursue the unknown or learn something new.

Passion - Passion is what gives us the motivation and drive to see things through. Quite often we will be working harder than any nine to five job and some days may feel like giving up but passion will keep us going.

Vision – Setting your sights high is a key to achieving big results. By putting it out-there the wheels have been set in motion for achieving it. Anything is possible!

Critical thinking – Being able to assess a situation and find a resolution to any issues is a skill that is beneficial to all author-publishers. Nothing is ever as bad as it first seems!

Confidence- When you believe in yourself, it makes it so much easier for others to believe in you too. When you are confident in your actions you will feel more empowered to reach your full potential and make magic happen for you and your business.

GROWTH
Build upon what you have already

Anyone can learn how to publish a book, but not everyone will have the skils around them to maximise the potential of their book. I want you to take a moment to acknowledge the skills and resources you have access to now and what you need to consider upskilling in or finding the perfect person for you to outsource to.

I strongly suggest that you learn what you are interested in learning and as you grow, build a team to outsource to.

What I have access to now...

What I need to learn or source...

Build a team to support your growth

You might not be thinking about it yet but building a team to support you will help you to publish more books effectively.

You do not have to bring in full-time employees yet but finding the right people who complement what you do and how you work are a valuable asset.

In my team I currently have:

In 2019 I will have a full time EA (Executive Assistant) join my team. In doing so I will be able to focus solely on my genius zone which is connecting with my authors, creating unique opportunites to facilitate growth and positioning my businesses aligned with their true potential.

What does your perfect team look like?

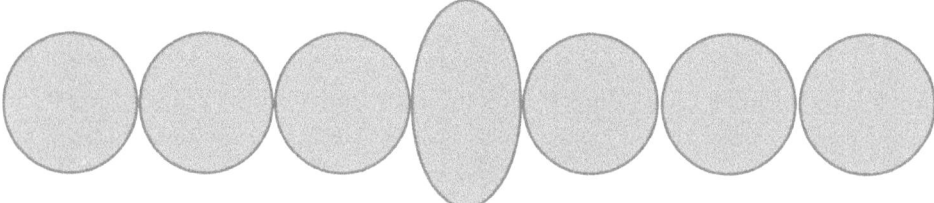

4 Publishing SUCCESS MILESTONES

Reach for the stars,

there's a beautiful view to behold.

MILESTONES
Four success milestones

There are many steps to publishing a book. If you consider them all at once it might feel overwhelming. That is why I always suggest that although you will know the bigger picture you should focus on the four main milestones individually and work through mastering each step to achieving those milestone moments on your journey.

These same principles apply to many aspects of life and when applied to publishing there is a greater chance of success and less chance of giving up on the process.

Write Great Words

I have said it before and I will say it again, make sure your words are as good as you can possibly make them before you move to production stage and definitely before publishing.

There is nothing quite as embarrassing as someone coming back on you because of discrepancies. Sometimes it is a writing style preference and that can be overlooked. Most readers are forgiving of first-time author errors but if you want to be respected as a serious author and have your book meet industry standards, having your words the best they can be is imperative.

That means:

Write your first draft

Rewrite

Send to Editor

Apply edits

Review

Proofread

Publish

You will feel so much more confident putting your book 'out there' when you know that your words are as tight as you can make them.

Design that book

Cover design

Let's chat cover design.

Your cover is what will give your book shelf appeal. No matter what genre you are writing in I highly recommend sourcing a cover designer.

There are lots of options depending on your budget. I have personally bought premade covers for fifty dollars and also commissioned designers for up to four hundred dollars.

There is something very special about seeing a cover designed especially for you with your name on it.

So unless you have design skills have a designer put together your cover.

You will:
- Sell more books.
- Be taken more seriously as an author.
- Be more confident promoting your book.

Tips for your cover design
- Only put YOU on a cover if you have a following.
- Don't have your name too small.
- Fit in with other books in your genre, but also stand out.

Interior design

Let's chat interior design.

There are different types of interior design, the main three being:
Novels, non-fiction and children's books.
Novels do not require much from a design perspective, however they do need to follow a universally recognised format that readers expect.
- Cover page
- Copyright page
- Dedication
- Acknowledgements
- Contents
- Body of the book
- Author information

Non-fiction books have so much room for design concepts. I recommend that you source a designer to do this for you as it will increase your credibility, ensure your reader has a more enjoyable experience and ensure that you have an industry standard book.

Children's books are fun and colourful. They do cost more to print but because of the low page count having a designer put them together is more cost effective. There are rules surrounding bleed for printers and dimensions need to be considered before your illustrator begins. I always create square children's books.

Publish with style

Think Big

Create a publishing environment that ensures the world knows about your impending book release. Think of innovative ways to stand out from the crowd. Take the back door because everyone else is lining up to get a ticket to walk through the front door.

Be ready to embrace oppotunities to speak, promote and share your book(s) with the world. Find your platform and project the best you can from there.

Build your press through positive intentions, doing good for yourself, your authors and illustrators and building beautiful bonds with industry contacts.

Go out of your way for your readers, they are the people who will determine your success. Have a business mindset and always approach any issues with a positive resolution mindset.

Keep your vibration high and your energy aligned with creating opportunities to reach readerships far and wide.

Cast your net as far as you can and each time you do you will reach new levels. Every reader has a network that they are connected to, every contact has people they connect with also. Build upon every connection and make it as positive as can be.

Spend time focusing your thoughts on your authorship or publishing press.

- Write down what comes to your mind.
- What audiences can you appear in front of?
- Who can you collaborate with?
- How can you grow your presence?
- Where are your readers?
- How can you increase your profile?

Position for success

Create a publishing environment that ensures the world knows about your impending book release.

Work as hard in building your marketing strategy as you did on writing your book.

You can position yourself well for success using these six strategies.
1. Bring your audience on the journey.
2. Write aligned with your brand.
3. Have a production schedule in place.
4. Be active in front of target audiences.
5. See the value in PR.
6. Have your book available for your audience to buy.

When positioned well your book will sell more copies.

Write below who your target audience is and where they are present online and in person.

knowledge notes

TOP TIPS

8 top tips for serious author-publishers

It is my hope that within the pages of this book you find information and inspiration.

It is set out as an introduction to each aspect of publishing where you can connect with each stage when you are ready to take action
at any given time.

Success will depend on the actions you take at each stage.

TIP #1: Focused intention and Knowing

When I first started publishing, I had a clear focus on the outcome I wanted to achieve: the opportunity to live my perfect life. A balance I was comfortable with that allows me to be a hands-on mum while fulfilling my ambitions.

I discovered my passion for sharing stories with the world. There is so much power in the written word. In a world where we multi-task on many levels the art of reading is an escape from that because when you read, you focus only on reading and so the words on those pages have a captive audience.

I found my way and made brave decisions to build a company that meant something, that had a positive impact. I made decisions channeled through my *Knowing* which is a step up from intuition. This concept allows us to make unwavering decisions because we *know* that the choices we make are aligned with our highest potential.

Feel it ~ Think it ~ Action it.

You can find out more about this life strategy in my book The Power of Knowing.

In business, as in life, having a clear vision of what you are setting out to do and WHY you want to do it, are crucial to success.

A focused intention ensures that you and your team are working towards the same outcome.

When time & circumstance align, magic happens

It is your job to set the intention and then take action when opportunity presents itself.

You will not control every step to the destination so let go of that need. The most successful people take action when the timing is right. They are confidently connected to their Knowing and you can be too.

Think for a moment what you want to achieve as an author and/or publisher. Write whatever comes to your mind straight away.

What do you hope to achieve?

TIP #2: Always learning.

I dicovered a passion for learning when I re-entered education as a mature student when I was twenty-five. I studied Humanities which had English literature components. I was like a sponge!

I realised the reason I did not enjoy school was because I wasn't interested in what they wanted to teach me. When I found what I really enjoyed learning about I was dedicated and learnt really fast.

Learning from experience, whether from personal experience or the experience of others, is an effective and more interesting way to increase your skills. Why not find a podcast or a blog by an industry expert you admire and learn from both their successes and failures.

It's amazing how much inspiration can come from listening to the stories of others who have gone before you. Be inspired but remember, create your own story, be a thought leader.

It is also OK to ask for help, you might be suprised by the valuable connections you will make by putting it 'out there'.

Pledge to yourself that you will always learn and grow and watch how interesting your journey becomes.

The more you learn the more you have to share and thus, the more income you can make by increasing your value.

What skills could I learn?

TIP #3: Find your Mentor

One of the best things I did for my business was to connect with a mentor.

Sourcing a mentor within your own field or the wider business arena who is willing to share their knowledge and experiences is an important step towards success.

Whie listening to the information your perfect mentor shares with the world is fabulous and is filled with value, it is important to remember that the information they share is focused on a wider audience. If they are having an impact with the masses, can you imagine what they can do for you when they work one on one?

I realised the potential of a mentor when I signed with Shevonne Joyce. I was really working so hard for very little money and she helped me realign and see my true worth. Instantly I was attracting ideal clients who valued what I had to offer and they were already committed to purchasing my higher end packages, which allowed me to do more for them.

A mentor does not want you to fail, it is in their best interest for you to achieve beyond your wildest dreams. They will go out of their way to share their knowledge and experiences with you to increase your success and the speed in which you achieve each level of success. They will work with you through the uncomfortable transitions.

Top tips for finding your perfect mentor:

- Write a wish list of people you would like to work with.
- Identify the qualities and strengths they have.
- What do you want to achieve with a mentor's guidance?
- Identify what is broken for you.
- Be prepared to invest to achieve future success.
- A mentor should challenge you to reach outside of your comfort zone.

Mentor wish-list

TIP #4: Publishing Schedules and Monitoring your Progress

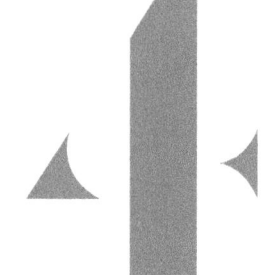

I am a very go-with-the-flow type of person. I believe very much in organically growing a business but one of the aspects of publishing that I value is having a publishing schedule.

It is important to keep track of each stage of publishing and ensure that you are hitting targets so that you can align your book with success on release.

Why do you think the bigger publishing houses have release dates way after they begin producton? It is because a lot of work goes on building momentum and raising the vibration of each book in anticipation for release.

There is a lot of value in having reviews circulating before release, especially from influencers.

My advice is to set a release date and work backwards from that point to the current date. Step out all of the stages and allocate a realistic time for each. Some might overlap and that's fine.

Monitoring progress as you go along will ensure that any hurdles or delays can be managed and overcome without hindering the release date or causing too much overwhelm.

Potential production schedule

Release Date:

# TIP #5: Build Your Team

When I first started out I did everything. I felt that I couldn't afford to take on any help. I outsourced editing because there was no way I could do it but everything else I learnt when I needed to.

It wasn't long before I was burning out and I discovered that I was costing myself money by tryng to do it all myself. Now I work more efficently by delegating what isn't my zone of genius so that keeps my vibration high and the energy surrounding each new release high also.

Every month I take time to stop and realign. Just like the wheels on a car need realigning, so too do our intentions. This is a good time to assess what is working, what is not and what needs to be embraced.

Your team should lighten your load, not add to it. Add the costs of your team to the costs of your services. The bigger the team you have around you, the higher the service you are offering.

It should be a win/win scenario all round.

Ask yourself some important questions:

- Is what you are taking on worth it from a time and energy perspective?
- Does it increase your presence and align with you achieving your future vision?

What could you outsource that would free your time to write and/or increase the value of your services?

TIP #6: Have fun!

When you are enjoying the journey of creating it will beam from you. Your energy will be higher and you will attract more positive things your way.

This goes for building your author-publisher brand as well as writing your book. People will want to join you on your journey, becoming your cheerleaders. They will be more inclined to talk about you, support your projects and send referrals your way.

When you think author-publisher what makes you smile?

TIP #7: Think and act like a business from Day 1.

Know that from day one you have created a business. It doesn't matter if you are an author publishing your own books or if you are setting up your own publishing house. Set the intention and own it like you deserve to.

The business of publishing might seem daunting but it doesn't have to be. In fact it is one of the primary reasons why big name authors stay under contract instead of branching out on their own.

It doesn't have to be this way. When you build a team around you to help lighten the load, then earning potential is high and writing time need not be jeopardised.

By setting this in place early it saves time transitioning your mindset later when you really need to have it in place.

It also helps you to be taken more seriously as an author-publisher. I always recommend that my author-publishers set up their own publishing imprint to represent them.

This encourages other businesses such as bookstores and distributors to invest the time into them as they are investing in themselves to build a platform.

There is success to be had so it's best to be prepared from the outset.

Notes :

TIP #8: Celebrate your wins and milestones.

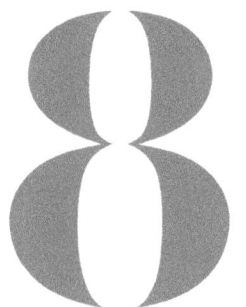

When we achieve something in business it is so importnat to pause and celebrate. You can do this in any way that suits you and quite often with a book it is a book launch. However I want to stress the importance of celebrating on a more intimate level for yourself and your family, who will have supported you as you reached your goal.

I reward myself in many ways. A movie night with my kids, a walk along the beach or a visit to the hairdresser. Maybe even a special dinner or a glass of wine, it all depends on what I achieve and where I am at within myself at the time. It is usually low key and family based as that is what makes my heart sing. My kids love watching me do my special happy dance when I get good news, haha!

How do you celebrate your wins?

_____
_____
_____
_____
_____
_____
_____

MANIFEST
Make it happen

So how do we take that dream and make it a reality? The first step in manifesting your ideal scenario is to open your mind to endless possibilities.

There are no limits to what you can make happen. Yes, challenges will come but they are not coming to block you, they come so that you can learn something new and evolve from that point. When you look at challenges as a positive then you will see the gates of success open wide for you.

Remember, it is OK to have your non-negotiables in life, these are the values and priorities that you don't want to compromise. I have mine and I manifest my success journey with these in mind.

To manifest successfully you will need to set a clear intention and banish any negative thoughts you might have surrounding it. When you think of what it is you want to achieve, feel what it will be like when you make it happen. Be grateful that you can pursue this goal and LOVE each step of the journey.

You are making magic happen in your life and the life of others; feel it and believe it!

You've written it before but it's time to write it again! What is your dream scenario?

It's now time to get real!
In the space below write down some ideas that you can build upon to make your dreams become a reality.

How will you turn your dream achievements into publishing reality?

THE STORY

How I built a publishing empire in five years.

PART ONE
The Early Days

'Nothing we learn in this world is ever wasted'
Eleanor Roosevelt

Looking at my background, publishing books would not have been foreseen in my future. Mind you, nobody could ever have dared to imagine what I would end up doing as I have always embraced opportunity and was always 'going somewhere'. I suppose I have always prepared myself to go that little bit further than anyone else. This has often gotten me into strife. During my teenage years and even during my twenties I found it hard to settle as I pursued exciting opportunity after exciting opportunity. I didn't often stop to think why, I just knew that I was following my heart and if it felt right, I did it. Areas of employment for me ranged from acting on stage, being a presenter, administration, managing a deli, supervising a high risk area in a meat factory and tutoring special needs students in the mental health sector. The list goes on and on and on ...

Early days

I was never good in school; I mean, I was smart but school didn't keep my focus. I went to an all-girls convent secondary school in Northern Ireland. I remember my parents being so proud that I had passed the entrance exam and earnt my place in the most prestigious girls' school in our county. I was very proud too but couldn't help but think that as I was the top of the class in most areas in the lower grade secondary school, was it better to be top at a lower level or mediocre at a higher level?

I was getting by at the grammar school, but as time went on I found it hard to hold my interest in the classes and I would get bored. I know now that I had made the wrong subject choices. For example, physics would have been a wonderful science to have under my belt but I never believed I was smart enough to choose it and so I chose biology, like my closer peers. Mistake! Looking back, I know that I would have benefited by being more philosophically based in my choices. Mind you, choices were limited as most of the subjects were compulsory.

To cut a long story short, my interests navigated more towards the social side of school and I would often wag class. At recess and lunch I would be found smoking behind the demountable, cigarettes I got from selling my dinner tickets. I rolled my skirt up high and I was becoming popular. I liked it, it made me feel good. Said skirt heightening would of course not take place until I was clearly out of view from both home and school.

Not so long ago an old friend from school contacted me on Facebook and said, 'Imagine if Mr Johns knew that you published your own book.' Mr Johns was my English teacher and he used to make me read out loud in class. I stayed back after class and asked him not to because it made me blush excessively and my mind would go in a tizzy. But he made me anyway so I got up and walked out of the class. That rebellious nature was not tolerated in this school. It was definitely the beginning of the demise of my educational prospects in secondary school. I couldn't wait to leave, get a job and start earning money.

I got a job in a tights factory checking stockings for holes. It wasn't glamorous but I thought I was the bee's knees earning 62 pounds a week. It didn't last long as the company went into administration. I got a job in my local town in the meat factory. This was my first experience of feeling that I was an integral part of a team and I loved it. Even though the job itself was totally mundane and mind numbing at times, the fun we had as a team and the camaraderie that was connected to it made me clock in every day.

Returning to Education

When my son was ready to start school I knew I couldn't do shift work because lifting him out of bed early on an Irish winter morning was not something I was prepared to do. So I resigned from my supervisory position and went back to school. I worked part-time while doing an access course which earned me acceptance for a place studying media at university, but it was not the right time. I had secured myself a perfect administration job that I enjoyed a lot and would open doors for me that surpassed any expectation I could have imagined.

I chose to study Humanities through an outreach university programme at my local college and I worked hard juggling everything for a few years but I did it and discovered a huge passion for learning.

At my part-time administration job, my manager brought to my attention a course that was available through a Dublin college that would require me to attend a weekend workshop in various locations around Ireland for the duration of a year. It was fully funded because it was aimed at training people to go out into the community and break down barriers that had been built up during the troubles in Northern Ireland. I was accepted and oh boy, did I learn so much during this time!

I was then offered a position teaching with a local college in their out centres. It was perfect and the same year I graduated with a Diploma in Humanities through the University of Ulster. I felt like the luckiest woman in the world and I was!

Turnaround

I endured a low time in my life that caused me to look inside. This was something I had never even considered when I was rallying through life at an excessive speed. Everything slowed down and simplified around me, it had to or I couldn't have handled it. Luckily I had worked in the mental health sector, and although I was not a nurse I knew what was happening to my mind and I also knew what I needed to do to get through it. I suppose the main thing was not to fear it! I put my new-found acting debut on hold and took each day as it came, focusing primarily on my children who needed me.

This time was invaluable in my transition to becoming a more aware person. I looked within and began to see the real Karen who was patiently waiting to make an appearance. I discovered that the opportunity for the most important personal growth comes when you reach your lowest point. When we are at our lowest point it often guides us to a state of contemplation and a quieter place where the craziness of before is past and with a clear mind, positive change can be worked towards. It's likened to pressing a rest button. This is quite often a blessing and I have come to realise that the Universe does these things when we refuse to acknowledge signs.

Discovering creativity

With my new-found appreciation for life I ventured forward at a slower pace, focusing purely on the simple things guided by my heart. We moved to Australia (when I was 35 weeks pregnant with my third child) to set up a new life for our family and when I arrived I felt so inspired. I began writing and illustrating children's books. It made my heart sing and my children loved it. I felt as if my puzzle was coming back together again. I was willing to be patient and go with it, not forcing it like I would have before.

> *Life is not about finding yourself, it is about creating yourself.*

I suppose without even knowing it I was reinventing myself. My son helped me choose the logo Mamma Mac's and I began to make the stories into homemade books. Even though this was not about achievement I decided to send my manuscript to a manuscript assessor called Angel Wings Manuscript Assessment that was based in Melbourne. When the assessment came back it was so encouraging, it was a great feeling. I didn't do anything with it at that time. I just began to share the love of my stories with my new Australian friend and her beautiful girls; she was always so positive when she spoke of my stories and I even created characters for her girls.

As I couldn't afford to send presents to nieces and nephews I would create a character for them, write them a story and do illustrations in their own personal book. As I grew I would computerise the books more. I remember the excitement when I discovered Microsoft Publisher; I could really bring my books to life. When my children were asleep I would sit with my Faber-Castell pencils and illustrate pictures for my next book project. I felt free and happy when I did this and seeing my son's face when I produced a new book for him was all the motivation I needed to keep going. I worked on about 30 books over this period in my life.

My husband saw my passion and wanted to support me as he believed in me so when I saw an advertisement in the paper asking, 'Do you want to publish your book, call us,' I did. We went to meet the guy in a coffee shop in Applecross (a fancy suburb in Perth, Western Australia). We had arrived early and so took a walk along the water's edge with our kids. I remember mentioning that if this guy was a rip off I would be able to do it myself someway. So off we went to meet him and he was charming, of course. To an enthusiastic aspiring author, what he had to offer was priceless, my book published and 500 copies to sell. The approximate price he gave me was $8000 and he had papers for me to sign there and then. I knew there would be hidden costs and looking back now I know I didn't have a platform to sell 50 books never mind 500. But something told me not to, it was too much money for my family at the time but I also felt that I was wiser for meeting with this guy. It was part of my journey a part of my Knowing there was another way.

'When there is a will, there is always a way!'

I decided to illustrate the books myself. I produced prototypes and secured a deal with local children's charity, Princess Margaret Hospital, to raise money through the sale of my books. They believed in me and agreed to me putting their name on my books. This was an amazing affirmation for me that others believed in my dream, but time and circumstance didn't align at that point and so I didn't pursue it further. I decided to send my manuscripts off to be considered by publishers. I collected a list of submission offices in Australia and I sent my books everywhere. This process takes a very long time and I learnt to be patient. I was very close to an offer of publication with a few of my manuscripts and so I knew that what I was writing was improving. The publishers were Wombat Books and Penguin.

(An interesting fact is that my first book Alphabet Job Buddies was almost published in 2010 by Wombat Books. In 2016 as a publisher I partnered with Novella Distribution and I was later to discover that Rochelle who owned Wombat Books also owned Novella Distribution. As this book is going to print for the second edition, Alphabet Job buddies is in production waiting release through Novella Disribution. It came full circle and the timing is perfect.)

Passion for writing

I joined a website called adoptamum.com which was founded by my beautiful friend. As I was living away from my mum I decided to join. WOW! I was introduced to a more loving metaphysical way of thinking. All of the women on the site shared support and love with one another. It was a virtual sanctuary, a home away from home, where we would meet and message each other and we never felt alone. I began to write little things and post them in the group. This led to me writing articles on things that inspired me at that time and I shared my philiosphy of life. I was changing so much at this time and I was absorbing information to support my new-found need for information. I showed some of my articles to the owner of the site and she was excited and asked if I would like to publish them there. They flowed and flowed and the owner published them. I was soon offered the position of 'Resident Writer'. This blew my mind! I was so excited; I couldn't believe that I was classed as a writer, someone who had walked out of her English class! I was given up on and I suppose I had given up on myself in that sense but now ... I had found a burning desire to write, write, write and I discovered that as I wrote I healed a little more.

Alignment

I soon realised that when everything shifts and aligns to make something possible it is quite magical and this is what happened when I chose to write my first novel. I had just given birth to my fourth child and was feeling very inspired. I had been becoming increasingly aware of the signals we are sent from time to time affirming that we are doing the right thing for us. I came across a writing challenge called NaNoWriMo that intrigued me. I had always been a person who excelled when challenged but I hadn't challenged myself in this way for a long time. The urge was there though and although many people would have commented that my timing was not great as I had a newborn, I knew the timing was perfect. I was at home and hey, what else would I be doing while breastfeeding?

What would I write about? The challenge was starting in a few days and I knew that I had to do it but was I being silly even considering it with only a few days to go? Then it happened. I was watching a bit of morning TV (something that I never did) and Whoopi Goldberg said something that resonated with me so deeply. I had experienced a miscarriage a few years previously and had not fully healed. She mentioned that it had been a visitor that came to help shift me back onto the right track in preparation for receiving the real gift. It was a truly big AHA! moment for me and I felt an overwhelming urge to share this message with the world. But how? Then I remembered NaNoWriMo and I knew that it would happen and it did. For 30 days I wrote 1667 words each day to achieve the 50,000 words required to win the challenge. I could not believe how it all flowed together. Every night the kids would go to bed easily and I would sit with my newborn, breastfeed her to sleep with one arm and single-handedly type my way to 50,000 words. The novel was finished; it was an emotional rollercoaster but I DID IT! What now?

My first publishing experience

OK, so what now? Would I send it to an array of publishers like I did with my children's manuscripts? That didn't sit well with me because I really wanted to bring it to the world now and I didn't want to wait years to have my book in my hand. I shared it with the people I love to get some feedback. My mum is my biggest critic and she absolutely loved it and my closest friend said that it 'just had to be published'. Then it happened, the site I was writing for sponsored the publication of my book. How lucky was I? My dream was becoming a reality.

I sent a self-publishing company my manuscript and the wheels were set in motion. I knew what I wanted for a cover but they told me the final decision was with them as they knew best. I thought this was strange. All was sailing along wonderfully, then I got calls from another department of the publishing house wanting me to get my book edited and it was going to cost more than the publication. This was a whopper, a total dream zapper. So how was this going to happen? I wanted the best for my book but I didn't want it to be changed. I loved my characters and their journeys, but I couldn't have it going out there with my name on it if it wasn't good enough to be read. After much deliberation, and with the support of my hard-working hubby, I chose to have it edited. To be honest I was surprised. I thought they would have changed heaps of it but they didn't, the lady just gently made it more readable.

The publishing company made a booboo and sent the unedited version to eBook format and I received an email from someone who bought it saying they found it hard to read and were finding it even harder to get any satisfactory response from the publisher. I contacted the publisher directly and they were not all that helpful and would not accept any blame. I asked them to reimburse the lady her money and offer her a free copy of the edited book. I still to this day don't know if they did that. They also wanted to charge me extra for different things and I felt it was becoming a real money pit; they didn't care about me or my book! I received phone call after phone call asking me to buy more books at a 'special price', marketing plans at a 'special price' and it went on and on. I received my first royalty letter stating I had sold an amazing five books and the publisher had earnt more royalties on each of these books than I did. It all just felt so WRONG! I did not feel in any way in control of my book.

The Publishing Venture

But as my quote said in the front of my book:

From all negative situations is the potential for a positive outcome.

I chose to focus on the positives with my book. I entered it into the Readers' Favorite book awards contest. It received a five-star review and was a finalist in the 2012 awards contest. I built up a rapport with the guys at Readers' Favorite because I believe so much in them. They work tirelessly and they give more than they receive. They do their job for the love of helping authors move forward in their career by making the process easier. They offer heaps of services from proofreading, to reviewing to book trailers etc ... the list is endless.

I had since also completed my second novel and things were exciting for me as an author. I noticed that affirmations were coming from all around letting me know I was doing the right thing. Being an author and selling books can be a full-time job so I researched what works and what doesn't and began to identify who was real and who wasn't. There are many people out there in the writing business who give more than they take in financial gain; to have a connection with people like this is priceless.

One of my friends from the website I wrote for approached

me early in 2011 and asked if I thought it would be possible to publish books. She was a fan of my work and I had mentored her to write her life story, 'In Search of My Soul'. After some research I discovered that the publishing company I had hired to publish my book used services that I could access myself and I could have complete control of my own book and royalties. Instead of earning $2 a book commission I could print my book for $4 to $5 and keep the rest for myself.

After a lot of work and research I worked it all out. I discovered that the US-based Ingram company Lightning Source had recently set up an office in Melbourne.

When time and circumstance align, magic happens.

I had nothing to lose and so I applied to Lightning Source to open an account as a publisher. This was what we needed as it provided us with access to worldwide distribution and we could print as few or as many books as we wanted. We could also place overseas orders by using their printing houses in both the UK and the US.

We were accepted as a publisher and we affiliated with Buildingbeautifulbonds.com who supported us and believed in us so much. As soon as we put up our logo a book submission came through with a truly inspirational story from an African orphan who dedicated his life to children through Shalom for Africa. True to our new-found vision, to publish inspirational stories, we had it edited and in 2014 published Prickle in a Dream within a month. This opened the floodgates and we collected inspiring stories for anthologies that we published over the next two years. We also created journals and with every book we learnt something new.

I soon discovered that every hurdle we faced was an opportunity to pause, learn something new and grow from that point with new skills.

We needed cashflow to grow and as all that I could commit to investing was $50, that is what I invested. I soon discovered that we needed a high design programme and so 'when there is a will, there is always a way', I partnered with iKoala.com to sell publishing deals to generate the income needed to make it happen.

Guided

From the outset I was guided through every step of the way. If I had thought of each step as a whole picture I would have been totally overwhelmed and ran away. Instead I chose to take it one step at a time and every challenge was an opportunity to learn and grow and oh boy, I love to learn new things.

I discovered my absolute passion for creating books. When one of our authors sends me a signed copy of their book thanking me for helping them make their dream become a reality, I beam with immense joy that I have been a positive influence on their publishing journey. It wasn't long before I had a shelf full. I was also astounded by the books that were attracted to me. Each of them was an aspiring author, setting out on their adventure.

Little achievements came along at exactly the right time to affirm that I was on the right path with Serenity Press.

A few of these to date are:

- In 2012, I was awarded acceptance into Stanford's Who's Who.
- In 2013, I was asked to be part of my first Perth-based weekend conference alongside Andrew Jobling.
- In 2013 InnerLight Publishing transitioned into Serenity Press.
- In 2014, Serenity Press was accepted as a publisher by APA.
- In 2014, we began our transition to becoming a traditional publisher.
- In 2015, I was a finalist in the Business Excellence category of Ausmumpreneur.
- In 2015, the wonderful Monique Mulligan joined our team. Her expertise is exceptional.
- In 2015, we had the most successful launch of our first romance anthology Rocky Romance at the inaugural Rockingham Writers Centre Book Fair.
- In 2015, we were given permission to gift Oprah a Serenity Press gift basket when she came to visit Perth.
- In 2016, I became an Ausmumpreneur Writing and Publishing expert, Ausmumpreneur Perth Ambassador and MC at their 2016 conference.
- We will continue to grow, think outside the box, support Australian authors and grow a strong Serenity Press team.
- 2016 was our greatest year of successes and we became a company.

*This list was compiled in August 2016 there is another list dating February 2019 in Part two

Attraction

I have used the universal Law of Attraction to bring to me exactly what it is that I want to experience in my lifetime. I am so convinced we all have the power to create anything that we want into our lives and when we connect this power to following our heart's desire, magic will happen! I decided to put my study cap on again and I earnt myself a certification as an advanced Law of Attraction practitioner. I have learnt that we are the only ones who limit ourselves. I apply this to my business principle and it allows Serenity Press to grow, albeit unconventionally, but most definitely with passion and determination.

> *When time and circumstance align, magic happens.*

I have always lived by this motto and now with my new-found appreciation for life I use it to be the best I can possibly be!

The Serenity Press initial vision was to share as many inspirational stories with the world as we possibly can but this has been further enhanced by offering authors the opportunity to publish their books in a positive way. It has now evolved further to become a traditional publishing company who creates amazing opportunities for authors.

We have created Making Magic Happen for authors who prefer to follow the self-publishing route and I am passionate that our authors will never feel negative about their book. Your book publishing experience deserves to be a positive one.

I have always known Serenity Press would be an inspirational story in itself; I know this because we have the truest of intention with every endeavour we undertake. We have made affiliations with wonderful people and the only way is up for us. We are a publisher with heart and as we grow, our authors grow too. We are a family and I am proud of what we continually achieve with our wonderful authors.

Part Two

Big Biz
August 2016 to February 2019.

'The meaning of life is to find your gift. The purpose of life is to give it away' Pablo Picasso.

Part one was written before August 2016. This was when things really took off for Serenity Press. Everything went next level when I won the Ausmumpreneur award.
Things were building momentum beforehand and the decision to play big and hire an Irish castle for a writers' retreat was just what my business needed.

So much has happened for me in the publishing arena that I know I have to share with you the huge deals that have presented themselves to us since then.

After winning the award we got so much PR. The best one was a full business page in an Irish newspaper. There I was, holding the award in my bright green dress accompanied by a full-page write up about my business success. I didn't realise that my dress was going to be such a feature. I had it especially designed and it was supposed to be blue but arrived in green. But everything happens for a reason and I rolled with it and was glad I did.

So back on deck and the focus was on the books we were producing and to keep things paid for I would offer services through my Making Magic Happen Academy.

Everything I made, I reinvested. It was my intention to build a million dollar company. That focus has never left me. I knew I had it in me and that I would make it happen by being courageous and focused on intention in the best possible way.

Monique Mulligan came on board as a partner, adding an amazing quality to the business. It may have lasted for a short time, but those two years were great and it was fabulous to share the journey with her, we had some amazing adventures.

We made a great team, we were very much a Yin and Yang connection. Two totally different approaches to doing things. And yet, it really worked. Monique brought stability and high quality, it was exactly what we needed at that time.
I chose to transition Serenity Press to a company in 2017 because of the liabilities connected to being two individuals. It was a total mindset shift. We had definitely stepped away from the early start-up phase towards becoming an independent press.
When the journey together was over, we parted in the most beautiful way. I know our friendship will last a lifetime, we both hold very high regard for each other and for the amazing things we achieved together for Serenity Press during this time.
It is through this partnership that I learnt one of my greatest lessons. It is that we all transition through seasons in our businesses and when we allow ourselves to transition *Knowingly* without stagnating somewhere we are not supposed to be for too long then that is where our true

Lots happened since 2016.

Amazing things happened with focused intention.

- Signed with Novella Distribution to bring our books to bookstores.
- First overseas print run for Writing the Dream inc free notebooks.
- A Bouquet of Love release
- November 2016 Writing the Dream release.
- Kate Forsyth signed with us for her fairytale retelling collection.
- Castle Retreat in Ireland.
- London Book Fair
- KiddyInks Lara and Tom
- Perth Writers Festival
- Signed with The Rights Hive
- Kindergo contract
- Signed Jane Talbot
- Signed Juliet Marillier
- KiddyInks school program a success.
- Signed Nadia King
- Signed Carolyn Wren's award winning collection of romances
- Released each of the 10 stories from our anthology as novelettes
- Rockingham Writers Convention panel.
- Vasilisa the Wise North American deal
- Made announcement of big changes.
- Speaker at Ausmumpeneur awards.
- Third in Global Ausmumpreneur awards.
- Met with Joanne Fedler and New South Books
- The Buried Moon signing
- Monique resigning
- 2018 retreat in Busselton
- Signed Kate Forsyth and Lorena Carrington for third book in series.
- Serenity Kids books
- Vasilisa the Wise places second in Readers Favorite book awards
- Destination Romance release
- Vasilisa Polish deal for International Women's Day

*so much more happened but this is a summary.

Yes, a lot of wonderful things happened. I do not share these successes to brag, I share them to show you what is possible when you have passion and purpose.

We had our first six-figure year in 2018 and the only way is up from this point. I will mention though that one of the things we are often not told is that when businesses have high yeilding years it is quite often a year of high investment.

Many things have contributed to this growth.
- Hard work and perseverance.
- Strategic partnerships.
- Keeping our vibration high.
- Building upon successful foundations.

Serenity Press will continue to organically grow and build upon the beautiful platform we have created. It is through maintaining a steady flow and creating an environment that is fertilised ready to flourish, run by a passionate heart.

With awesome authors and illustrators we will continue to produce high quality beautiful reads for current and future generations.

I look forward to seeing where the next few years bring us. This is how I built my publishing press in just five years. If this is the path you choose, I wish you every success and hope that I can join you on your journey.

5 tips
How to fit writing into your life

1 — SET A CLEAR INTENTION
When you set a clear intention opportunity to write finds it way to you.

2 — MINDFULLY WRITE FOR 21 DAYS
Create a habit for writing! A little every day = words down on paper.

3 — ALLOW YOUR FIRST DRAFT TO FLOW
Writing flows easiest when you use YOUR voice.

4 — SCHEDULE WRITING TIME AS IF IT IS A BUSINESS CALL

5 — STEP BY STEP = SUCCESS
Take it one step at a time, write in manageable chunks.

YOUR STORY

Believe to achieve the highest heights.

Make success inevitable.

Start with where you are and make it magical!

CONCLUSION
Final words

In this book, we have covered the key elements of publishing and I have shared my journey in the hope you will better understand that you need to embrace YOUR journey with open arms.

You can be inspired by others on your journey but it is important that you weave your own web so that you create a legacy to be proud of. That is where true lasting success resides.

Publishing can be as complicated as you want it to be. I suggest you start from where you are, take steps forward always and when you face a challenge, pause, learn what you need to and evolve from that point.

To your publishing success!

EDUCATING AUTHOR-PUBLISHERS ACROSS THE GLOBE
ONLINE LEARNING PLATFORM includes:

> Access to Members Hub (inc member exclusive training, resources and expert interviews)
> Facebook group membership including mentoring from Karen Mc Dermott.
> Everything Publishing Ultimate Publishing Guide Book and Workbook.
> One on one mentoring session to get you on the right track for YOUR publishing journey.
> Access to opportunities outside of the group.
> Regular interactive facebook lives.
> A community of fellow Author-Publishers.
> Monthly networking

Everything Publishing Academy Masterclass

Our feature presentation is
How to be more successful in your industry of choice through publishing a book.

Contact us for more info: hello@karenmcdermott.com.au

www.everythingpublishingacademy.com

The No. 1 Global Community
for
Author - Publishers.

Education
Opportunity
Community
Member's Hub
Workbook
Expert interviews
Training
Guidance

www.everythingpublishingacademy.com

www.ingramcontent.com/pod-product-compliance
Lightning Source LLC
Chambersburg PA
CBHW062110290426
44110CB00023B/2773